Mahlon D. Collins

The common Sense of Bible Salvation

Mahlon D. Collins

The common Sense of Bible Salvation

ISBN/EAN: 9783337171469

Printed in Europe, USA, Canada, Australia, Japan

Cover: Foto ©ninafisch / pixelio.de

More available books at **www.hansebooks.com**

M. D. COLLINS.

THE

COMMON SENSE

OF

BIBLE SALVATION

BY

M. D. COLLINS.

PHILADELPHIA, PA.

CHRISTIAN STANDARD COMPANY, Ltd.,
PUBLISHERS AND BOOKSELLERS,
921 Arch Street.

INDEX.

INTRODUCTION.

SO far as an introduction may have the nature of an apology I am afraid of it. I learned years ago, in my ministry, that to apologize in the performance of a religious duty was to run the gauntlet of many dangers. The first of these dangers was that of overstating the case. So, for a long period, I have skipped apologies. The reason I have written this book is the same for which I preach a sermon. I felt its truths and their fashion come to me in much the same way that my sermonic truths come. Having the truth a "fire in my bones," it sought outlet, and this book is the gateway.

The truths of full salvation need "line upon line, precept upon precept" of statement, because of false and perverted teaching, and because of the "dullness of ears and the hardness of heart of the people." It is a characteristic of Holy Spirit times that many shall run to and fro and knowledge shall be increased. We rejoice to be one of the "runners." May the knowledge of freedom from sin be increased until the last laboring child of the kingdom shall be "free indeed!" Toward this consummation may this little messenger be a herald and contribution!

5

I.

COMMON SENSE.

Uncommon sense is much sought for. Common sense has few pursuers. We have fallen on times when people are after the extraordinary, the unusual. People wish to be extraordinarily rich, learned, great, or in some particular beyond those about them, while the ordinary fields are quite forsaken. Yet the pathway to the permanently and valuable extraordinary, is to be found by way of the ordinary. But this is an apparently dusty old way, and seems not very attractive.

Common sense is the sense we use in every-day affairs, about common things. Take twelve average men, selected at large, just as they come, in the ordinary places in life, and submit a question to their unbiased judgment, and their conclusion would be the verdict of common sense. Common sense is the easy, unforced, unstrained sense which comes without labored effort. This was the reason the "common people" heard Jesus "gladly." He spoke in their language. Do you remember His ever making a classical quotation in sermon or address? He was the simplest and plainest teacher that ever trod the earth. He spoke of young ravens, sparrows, fish, hens and chickens, dry grass, green trees, foxes and their holes, lilies, sand, corn, sheep, pits, ditches, oxen, clay, spittle, eating, drinking, purging, vomiting, dogs, hogs, and innumerable common things in life. Surely in the direct simplicity of His method, "never man spake like this Man." He differs from the Scribes and Pharisees, the professional teachers of every age, in that they speak after the schools. He speaks after nature. God made man just right at the beginning; sin denaturalized him; salvation gets him as near back to these normal orders as it is possible to restore him. Salvation, full and free, is the frictionless, easy, happy, harmonious life. God gives it to all. Nay, He is offering it "without money or price." Common sense says accept it, everybody.

II.

SALVATION—WHAT?

Salvation is deliverance from danger. The baby fell into the rain barrel, and would have drowned, but mother saw the little feet following the rest of the baby into the depths. With a scream she ran and rescued it. She saved it from death by drowning. Saved it from present peril, and future death. Is the baby any dearer now, as it lies in mother's arms, fondled and kissed, with oft repeated expressions of affection, than it was before the adventure in the rain barrel? No, but this occasion has served to show the affection which lay in the mother's heart all the while.

Sin is a present danger, and sure death to the soul, in the end. Salvation is deliverance from sin; the danger and death-dealing assault upon the soul. It is not getting to heaven; that is where saved people go at last. It is not joining the church; that is a very natural and likely thing for saved people to do. It is not faith in the Bible or even faith in Jesus; that is what people do to be saved; "Believe on the Lord Jesus Christ and thou shalt be saved."—Acts 16: 31. It is not something we do; it is

9

something done for and in us. The condition is "Believe
on the Lord Jesus Christ." The salvation is the act of
God by which we are delivered from that which endangers
our case. "Thou shalt call His name Jesus, for He shall
save His people from their sins."

Salvation is present, continuous, and final. Present
salvation is that which a sinner may have now on the condition of "faith on the Lord Jesus Christ."

Continuous salvation is this rescue extended through a
period of time and a succession of events. How may present salvation be continued? God has covenanted to
continue to save us upon the same conditions upon which
He rescued us in the first place. "As ye have therefore
received Christ Jesus the Lord, so walk ye in Him."—Col.
2: 6. When I instantly and fully obeyed my conviction
of what I ought to do, then He immediately saved me.
And so I shall keep saved by instant and full obedience to
the light of conviction I have. In what does present salvation from sin consist? In deliverance from the guilt
of sin I saw and felt was upon me. "He that believeth
not is condemned already, because he hath not believed
on the name of the only begotten Son of God."—John 3:
18. In deliverance from the dominion of sin: "For sin shall
not have dominion over you; for ye are not under the law,

but under grace."—Rom. 6: 14. From the power of sin by legal force to sell us out of our rights in the family of God. Our child rights in the family of God are by sin legally forfeited, and we inherit only when we serve. If we sin we are children of the devil, and can inherit only on that line. But salvation cancels the mortgage of sin, restores the lost patrimony, and puts us on the line of our inheritance again. "If sons, then heirs." We are now on the line to get heaven by family right. Most people are trying to secure heaven as a reward of good behavior. We get capacity by doing right; but we get heaven by inheritance. It is the love gift of the Father to the family. We do right because we are right, and being born from above we become citizens of the heavenly country by "birth from above."

If our pedigree is clear we shall have heaven by the will of God. Will a regenerate soul go to heaven? Yea, verily, there is no other outcome for him. What need then of entire sanctification? The need lies in the fact of the nature of heaven. It is holy, and only holy ones are at home in holy places. Regeneration makes heaven possible. Entire sanctification makes us "meet to be partakers of the inheritance of the saints in light."—Col. 1: 12. There is no question but that we must be holy before we enter heaven, for "without holiness no man shall see the Lord." There is no question but that every child of God is born to a perfectly holy life. He has the pledge and prophecy of this in what is done for him at every stage of the salvation process. What is done is perfectly done, so far as it goes. He is perfectly regenerated; no needed retouching of this work of the Holy Spirit. He is perfectly justified from all his past sins, as completely as though he had never sinned. He is perfectly adopted; not taken into the back kitchen, promoted after a time of good behavior to the sitting-room, and then permitted to enter the parlor. But at once and for all he is taken into the full fellowship of the Father's adopting love.

But many a child is born to an inheritance he never enters fully upon or enjoys. It is said hundreds of thousands of pounds lie in the Bank of Scotland awaiting claimants by rightful heirs; many of whom, no doubt, have perished in want in distant lands, not because they did not have rights to the future, good and true, but because they did not do that which was needful in order to become "partakers" of their legacy.

What, then, is full salvation? It is deliverance from "sin which dwelleth in me"—the "carnal mind"—the "old man." Reason as we may; adopt what theory of sin we choose, every regenerate soul finds out subsequent to his conversion that there is something in him which constantly, and at times violently, endangers his standing in the life produced in him by regeneration. Something in him, not temptation from Satan or the world, not merely natural appetites, but something in the appetite which does not belong to normal appetite, which is liable and tends to flash up like powder and blow away position gained by days of labor; or like a wild torrent tends to bear away before its wild tide the whole structure of life born in them by the Holy Spirit. Call this what we may, or let it be nameless, it is the common experience of the best cases of converted men and women that they seriously encounter this oppressing force and long and pray for deliverance from it. Here lies the issue. Can we by the same process of faith on the Lord Jesus Christ be delivered from this inner somewhat that gives us so much trouble? The Bible says we can—and this is what we mean by full salvation. Salvation meeting the last element of our sin difficulty.

What is final salvation? It is the obtainment of the remotest result of the Calvary purchase. What yet remains after present, continuous, and full salvation? The body is yet to be saved from corruption, ignominy and death. The mind is yet to be saved from infirmity, imperfection, and deception. When the body is raised in "incorruption" and made like unto "Christ glorious body;" and when the mind is delivered from all the incubus and paralysis sin has brought on us, then shall we have the full fruition of final salvation. A glorious body, a glorified mind, and a holy soul reunited forever shall enter on the reaping of the glorious harvest of eternal life.

III.

BEING AND DOING.

The Bible and common sense go together. The sacred
book and prayerful self-examination discover that the difficulty with our lives is a twofold one. We do wrong, and
we are wrong. The clock cannot keep correct time until
it be right within. When right within, the outside will
be true to the movements of the sun. "Make the tree
good and the fruit will be good also," said the Master
Teacher. We have a history of wrong doing. "We have
sinned and come short of the glory of God." This history and fact can be remedied. How? Pardon for the
guilt. Regeneration, turning the life from, to God; justification, giving a new relation to law.

But after this all agree; Bible, theologian, and experi-
mentalist, that while the regenerated soul does right if
he maintains his new relation, and as long as he maintains
that relation, yet he does so against an internal bias that
shows him conclusively that he is yet internally wrong.
The trend and tendency is to go wrong. Held under, so
submerged at periods as to be not at all recognized, as
the tide of the happy, joyous, new life sweeps on, yet again
and again appearing and contesting that new life at every

15

point of its movement. All agree as to the facts. Great the diversity of remedies or application of remedy and hope of recovery. But all agree as to the internecine war. The rebellion is conquered, but reconstruction is not yet complete. Ku Klux yet are in the country.

All agree that depravity survives regeneration, and is found as a live factor in truly regenerated lives. "All," we said, all the authorities, all the theology, all the authoritative statements of the theologies agree. Here and there are individuals who disagree, but the concensus of the church militant is a unit, and has been for eighteen centuries. Theories of remedy are varied, but the great mass, those who have tried it by the Bible way, almost in the one voice cry out that by the same simple way by which the cloud of guilt was dissipated may the stain of inner pollution be washed clean away.

Those who have had the clearest experience of the first work are they who also have the most transparent experience of the second. The Bible promises, and repeated experiences demonstrate, that just as we are justified by faith from the guilt of past sin, so by the same kind of faith in the same atoning merit of the blood of Jesus, we may be delivered from the conscious inbeing of sinward trend in our moral natures.

IV.

WE OUGHT TO BE HOLY.

God commands us to be holy. "Be ye holy, for I, the
Lord your God am holy."—Lev. 19: 1, 2. And that this
command applies to the fullest definition of holiness, under the dispensation of the Holy Ghost, is manifest from
the fact that Peter reiterates it in his latest, and one of
the latest writings of the New Testament. This command
is not to "aim at holiness" as a distant goal, no more than
the command "thou shalt not steal" is a command to aim
at honesty as a final achievement. All agree that holiness
is the ought-to-be of moral status for all men. This being
true, and God having provided for its immediate obtainment by faith in the all-potent atoning blood, holiness,
becomes in the creature true loyalty to God. God is my
creator, lawgiver, judge. I am His by creation, providen-
tial preservation and redemption, and I ought be His
by glad, free, and full consecration of every living power
to God. He commands me to "be holy:" I ought to obey.
Holiness is loyal obedience on the part of the subject.
But not this alone. The divine side of this transaction is
that which makes holy. As soon as the loyal subjects of

17

my wholly redeemed nature return to God in true, entire consecration, then the Holy Ghost comes and occupies His chosen residence ("Ye are the temple of the living God"), and that act of occupation by the Inabiding Spirit coming and filling the soul is that which sanctifies and makes holy.

Holiness is loyalty to my neighbor. I cannot "love God whom I have not seen, and hate man whom I have seen." The two relations are "like." I must "love God with all my heart and my neighbor as myself." Holiness is loyalty to myself. I was made for God. "The chief end of man is to glorify God and enjoy Him forever." I cannot do this unless I be holy. God is holy, and unless I am in harmony with Him I shall be forever striking the bucklers of the Almighty. As truly as a locomotive is made for a track, with a certain kind of rail, just so many feet and inches apart, so I was made for God. I fit nowhere else; I run smoothly no other place in life. It is not a question of theologies, theories, or this or that; it is a constitutional question. Being made for God, I am, by the construction of my nature, unfitted forever for any other place in the universe. There is nothing else like God in this universe, so there is nothing else to fit to but God. Garfield said: "If a man will get so that he can sleep well with himself, then there is nothing in the universe can disturb his slumbers." But you can never "sleep well with yourself" until every faculty responds in harmony with God.

V.

CAN I BE FULLY SAVED NOW?

I can be what I ought be, or God demands what I cannot fulfil. But He is just, and does not anywhere require of me what He has not given me power to do or be. He commands me to repent of sin and return to the pathway of obedience, and by His grace always guaranteed the honest soul, I can. He commands me to "love Him with all my heart and mind, and soul, and my neighbor as myself," and by the same grace of God I can, for He has promised "to circumcise my heart, and the heart of my seed to love Him with all my heart," etc. If grace can save at all, it can fully save. If it can deliver me from any of my sins, it can deliver me from all my sins. Sin is all of one fibre, and that which can eradicate one part of it can take out all. Also that which is true of all sin at any time is true now. If ever the grace of God will be effective to meet the whole case of my need, it is equal to meet it now. Grace, or the faith which renders that grace available, will never be any more efficient than it is now. There is no faith but now faith, and there is no promise of grace but now. This, then, is not a question for the metaphysicians or theologians merely, but it is a question of fact. "Stephen was a man full of faith and of the Holy Ghost," whether any one can explain it or give us the true philosophy or not. The gospel is a record of fact leaving the ages to give us the philosophy. If my philosophy must measure my facts, or experiences, my measure of salvation is small indeed.

The testimony of the whitest souls in the Christian ranks, through the ages, is no mean factor in the settlement of this question of the measure of salvation faith may compass now; as Bishop Janes said, "What are we to do with the testimony of Stephen Olin, Bishop Hedding, Wilbur Fisk, and thousands of others who give as clear and unequivocal testimony to holiness as a second distinctive experience wrought in the soul subsequently to regeneration?" And this query will not down at the philosophizing of every or any man. The list might be easily indefinitely extended from John Wesley and Hester Ann Rogers to John S. Inskip and Phoebe Palmer. These give as intelligent a testimony, and as beautiful a life, attesting regeneration, as any in the whole court of Christian hosts. They are as competent as any to give testimony on the spiritual life, and there is a marvelous unanimity in their testimony. If testimony is good for anything, theirs counts with its full weight for holiness as a second definite work of grace in the soul. He is a brave man indeed who can stand and gaze along the line of this column made white in the blood of the lamb, and declare "They no doubt sincerely thought they were delivered from the carnal mind, but they were mistaken."

Here and there men and women have been mistaken on vital matters, but sooner or later the mistake is discovered and corrected. But here is a mistake, if error it be, that has continued in unbroken line and increasing numbers for centuries, and men and women embrace it as earnestly now as ever in the years. I know of no more competent class to answer my query, and from none comes a more unequivocal answer than this blood-washed company who, when I ask them, Can the soul be delivered from the carnal mind, through the blood of Jesus, applied to the believing soul by the Holy Ghost? responded with a voice that thunders down the ages, "Aye and Amen."

VI.

HOW KNOW IT?

Just as I know any other fact of experience. I knew I was a guilty soul, when I was in rebellion against God. I knew it, not by reason, but even in spite of and against my strongest protest of reasoning. I knew it when the burden was lifted and gone. I knew that the same I who had long ago gone as a cart beneath its sheaves was now disburdened and ran, yea, flew with alacrity and delight along the way I had so long shunned and avoided as a shady and sombre way. I knew it also by the direct witness of the Spirit that I now stood in filial and loving favor with God as His reconciled child. And the further and subsequent experience was just as clear to my consciousness, and as satisfactorily attested by the Holy Ghost, as a child of God, walking in the favor and fellowship of my heavenly Father, I knew there was something in my interior life that antagonized the regenerative life received at my pardoning. This something, which at first I was surprised to find, then made me solicitous to know as to its nature and right to be there. I found it wonderfully described in the Bible under such terms as "sin which dwelleth in me"—the "carnal mind enmity against God" —the "old man"—"old Adam," etc. This I found as I introspected my soul under the best light, in the most secluded hour of my soul opening to God. At times how burning the consciousness! How intense the struggle to down it! To persuade myself it was a temporary disorder! But the more I opened my whole being to God and prayed for light, the more clearly I saw there was a deep-seated, hereditary something that warred against the Spirit in my soul and kept up internecine discord. Deny that I am a competent witness, but too deeply written in my soul is the memory of those days of inner self discovery under the light of the Holy Spirit to be overthrown or dissipated by any system or process of philosophizing. Then there came a crisis. I became desperate. I felt there ought to be help for an honest soul. I sought it. I cried to God for it. I found, at last, certain passages of Holy Writ marvelously expressing my soul hunger as of some one who had gone over this same road before me. "Create in me a clean heart, O God"—"Wash me and I shall be whiter than snow"—"I am undone, I am a man of unclean lips." Then I cried in the face of heaven. My cry was heard. My floundering, desperate soul caught hold of this plank: "If we walk in the light as He is in the light, we have fellowship one with another, and the blood of Jesus Christ his Son cleanseth us from all sin." I clasped it with both hands, and it supported me. In a few hours it bore into a quiet harbor, where my soul has been marvelously resting all the years since. Am I mistaken? Some say "I am, and that while the uplift is good for the soul, and the epoch in soul progress one to be desired, but that the soul was not really delivered from the carnal mind." This can only be by stages, and long contests, and steady growth, by experience with the subtle foe, and then along the drive somewhere I may at last be delivered. Well, if the power to deliver is the blood of Jesus, I will still hold this as efficient and sufficient now as ever it will be. As dear old John Wesley reasoned "If by faith, why not now?" But to the facts again. Let us give allowance for some souls that are rather given to over-enthusiasm, and may have been deluded; but what shall we do with the great numbers of intelligent, clear-brained, honest-hearted souls like Hedding, Hamlin, Asbury, Abbott, Foster and Joyce, and a thousand others who come rushing in at memory's gate, all gladly testifying to the one thing. Shall we say these are all mistaken? These did not know what they were talking about? Were Thomas M. Eddy and Bishop Janes mistaken? Are they the class of men who take up a hurried conclusion, and then find they have claimed too much? Was Dr. Keen, on his dying bed, when he declared "the gospel of full salvation he had preached to others was all and more than he had declared it to be," but laboring under a mistaken idea as to his spiritual condition before God?

It is said "some have supposed they were delivered from depravity who later on found they were mistaken, and the carnal mind again asserted itself." Well, other "some" have supposed they were delivered from the "old man" of sin, and in the face of testings severe, and after years of deliberation, still declare God has kept them in sweet and steady victory so that they have not had any uprising of the carnal heart antagonizing the spirit of God in them. So that over against the "some" who found they had been mistaken we put the other and larger "some" who still declare they were not mistaken. This large and growing company find such Scriptures as this very spontaneously, and fully express their now state before God and men: "Knowing this, that our old man is crucified with him that the body of sin might be destroyed that henceforth we should not serve sin."—Rom. 6: 6. It is too late in the day to philosophize away so rugged and fire-tested experiences as this full salvation brigade present.

It has been asserted that "the Holy Spirit is nowhere promised in the Scripture as the witness to any state but that of adoption." We grant this so far as exact and specific language is concerned. But do we believe nothing taught in the Bible save that which is specifically and definitely named in so many words? Surely such a position will not be claimed by a Bible teacher. The Bible does teach that, "Now we have received, not the Spirit of the world, but the Spirit which is of God: that we might know the things that are freely given to us of God."— I Cor. 2: 12. If full salvation is the free gift of God out of the virtue of the atonement of Christ, then it is clearly within the purview of this passage, and certified to the soul by the Holy Spirit of God.

"Hereby know we that we dwell in Him and He in us, because He hath given us of His spirit."—I John 4: 13. This refers to the promise made by Christ before His departure, of the "promise of the Father," which came on Pentecost "purifying their hearts by faith." From that day one characteristic of holiness has been the fact that the Triune God abides in a purified soul. The permanence of His presence is distinctive from the earlier experiences of the salvation life, and not the permanence of maturity, but a permanence that began with the sanctifi-

cation of the soul as by a sudden introduction into a state
of permanent indwelling of the Comforter.

VII.

WILL WE KEEP SAVED?

Keeping fully saved is no more difficult or uncertain than keeping saved at all. If we can keep ourselves in the favor of God in pardon, we can in entire sanctification. "Now unto Him that is able to keep you from falling, and to present you faultless before the presence of His glory with exceeding joy, to the only wise God our Saviour, be glory and majesty, dominion and power both now and forever. Amen."—Jude 24: 25. He is as much disposed to "keep us" as He is "able" to do it. The great question is not so much what we can do in the way of diligent and vigilant watchfulness as it is a query as to whether we shall maintain our faith-unity with the Omnipotent Keeper.

"If we walk in the light as He is in the light, we have fellowship one with another, and the blood of Jesus Christ his Son cleanseth us from all sin." Can we do this? Well, the probabilities of success are greater with a perfect faith than with an imperfect one. The chances are manifold more when depravity is eliminated than when this subtle quicksand still underlies the soul. True, there is still the great enemy of the soul—Satan—who can still

31

assail the soul, and will likely dog us to the end. True, natural appetites, in a weakened body, and impaired mind still are to be considered. These must be "kept under" and brought into subjection. True, free agency still abides, and we can sin, as a moral probability, so long as we are probationers; but thanks be unto God there is no power can compel us to sin. So that on every hand we shall still need

> "To watch and fight and pray
> The battle ne'er give o'er;
> The work of faith will not be done
> 'Till we obtain the crown."

All the helps to growth in grace, in wisdom, power, love, will now come to the soul who would "be faithful unto death." "The righteous also shall hold on his way, and he that hath clean hands shall be stronger and stronger."—Job 17: 9. The soul, in a life of holiness, will find faith in Jesus' power and willingness to save, becoming the fine art of life. The query is turned from "What can I do?" to "What can I trust Jesus to do for me?"

Falls there may be, "but if any man sin we have an advocate with the Father Jesus Christ the righteous." That we may fall at any point this side the "pearly gate," does not prove that the holiness confessor did not have what he supposed any more than falling from regeneration proves that the subject was not "born from above." The ability and disposition of God, the all-sufficient, is guaranteed to keep those who "look unto Jesus;" and many are so kept, which establishes the rule, which is further confirmed by the exception.

VIII.

GROWTH.

The laws of growth as related to the permanency of Christian life are too little apprehended and conformed to. Into the state of grace we are introduced by the act of God. Regeneration and entire sanctification are produced by the act of God. The Methodist catechism clearly puts the Bible teaching when it says: "Sanctification is the act of divine grace whereby we are made holy." "I am the Lord that doth sanctify you."—Ex. 31: 13. "The very God of peace sanctify you wholly."—I Thess. 5: 23. Insensate things as "pots and vessels" are sanctified in the elementary sense of being set apart for holy uses, but when the term is applied to free agents and immortal souls, it carries the much larger and wider idea of the incoming of God into the consecrated vessel, and by this incoming, approving and appropriating act, rendering the intelligent vessel a "partaker of the divine nature," and so be not only relatively holy as a thing, but really holy as an intelligent receiver of the divine sanctity. Get this Bible idea clearly in mind, and you are thus ready to consider the relation and office of growth. The graces of the spirit are

divine bestowments. Nor do they grow. We grow in
them. We do not make the graces larger, but we become
larger in capacity for them, and flexibility in their movement. "We are God's husbandry," literally, "God's farm."
He furnishes seed and sunshine, and we grow, and produce His crop. He breaks up the fallow ground of our
hearts, seeds us down with the clover of His love, and we
produce "fruit unto holiness."

We grow in power. Power is of God. He is the
source; we the media. We grow in ability to use and
manifest power. He does not make us reservoirs, but
wires of communication. We cannot store power, but
grow in knowledge of our resource, and habit of depend-
ence upon its availability. We grow in harmonious action
and smoothness of movement. At first the wheels and
pinions of our spiritual machinery are rough, and do not
move smoothly and evenly. But time and action will give
grace and facility to our movement. All the graces are
given full-fledged, but we have to learn how to use them,
like a boy who for a Christmas present has received a box
of toy carpenter tools. They are all then bright, new,
and perfect; but of many of them he has but small idea
how to use them for result. Their possession is his, and
he is happy in that fact; but what he can do with them,

and how many excellent things his busy hands and thoughtful brain can fashion with them, he has yet to learn.

In this sense we are to "add to our faith virtue, and to virtue knowledge," etc., not in a mathematical way, adding one at a time, these graces, until we at length secure a full complement. But this word "add" in II Pet. 1: 5, has the meaning of facility in using. Here growth has an important office in developing facility in using the graces. They are not alone given for ornament, but for practical and vital use. So we are to learn to use faith so as to increase its own appropriating power, and to enlarge its compass. The dexterous pianist learns to reach, by constant application, nearly twice as far with his fingers on the keys, as he could at his first effort. We are to learn how to use courage. That fearlessness the liberated soul feels who bounds out from under the load of carnality, which has made his spiritual progress so slow-paced hitherto; he must learn to use it so that it will not seem self-sufficiency or brassiness, and so hinder instead of help usefulness.

So we merely indicate the field of growth. But a word more as to growth from another point of observation. We must grow. We can maintain no state of grace attained

but by going on beyond it. This is the law of spiritual
progress: "Unto him that hath, unto him shall be given,"
or he that uses what he has as a wise investor shall have
more. "But from him that hath not"—does not use—
"shall be taken that which he hath."

Thus we see that instead of entire sanctification, or any
other state of grace, being a point at which we can receive
no more, it is the point of true spiritual acquisitiveness;
at which we can and do receive in a ratio hitherto never
attained. A finite soul will never cease to grow. The
unpicturable pattern of divine excellence will ever be before it, toward which it will be reaching out forever and
ever. Let us heed this ever constant need of the soul,
conformity to the laws of growth.

Growing things are tender, as you see in the tendrils of
a live and luxuriating grape vine. So the soul, under
grace, will grow in tender appreciation and apprehension
of the nature and mind of Christ and Christly things.
Growing trees reach deeper and higher—grow up and
down. So we must be "rooted and grounded in love," and
grow up into Christ, the living head in all things.

IX.

TRIAL.

The trial to which the Christian is subject is twofold. First, from assault by Satan who solicits to evil. From the Lord, directly or permissively, for the sake of developing temper or flexibility, and for the sake of usefulness. Solicitation to evil is always from either a depraved heart or from Satan. When depravity is removed by the cleansing blood, then solicitation to evil is always external, from the devil or his agencies. From the latter we cannot be freed so long as we are probationers. The very name implies trial with possibility of yielding to fall.

Some have imagined that when entirely sanctified, they could not or would not be solicited to evil any more. No greater mistake could be made. The devil wastes no ammunition, and so but superficially assaults the half slumbering Christian. But you go over fully to God, and get filled with the Holy Ghost, and so become a real live, aggressive factor in the kingdom of Christ, and the devil will awake and assault you with a violence that will surprise you. He never massed his forces and taxed his re-

sources so to accomplish his ends, as when Jesus invaded
what He claimed as His territory, this earth.

Several things may be learned to our profit from the
scene in the wilderness immediately following His baptism.
The record says "being full of the Holy Ghost, He was
led up of the Spirit into the wilderness to be tempted of
the devil."—Luke 4: 1.   It is when we are "filled with the
Holy Ghost" that our fiercest contest with Satan comes.
All previous contests with him have been but skirmishes.
Satan fell from purity, and like all other backsliders he is
chronically doubtful of the stability of any soul.   From
the backslider you have that "every man has his price."
Though very crafty and ingenious, yet he is still very
ignorant of spiritual resources.   Though mighty he is
not almighty.

The first assault Satan made on the second Adam was
the old one by which he trapped the first Adam—by appeal
to appetite.   A pious soul who has been delivered from
the carnal mind, or the sinward bent in appetite, may yet
fall as Adam did through allowing appetite to lead beyond
the divinely fixed boundary thereof.

Here is where some fail in a proper definition of depravity.   They do not discriminate between a legitimate
appetite which may be normal and good in itself, and that

inherited perversion in appetite which causes it to tend to sin, and that continually. So Satan appealed to hunger in Jesus. Adam the first fell by misbelief of God. Jesus stood by the obedience of faith, which is faith of soul. Secondly, Satan appealed to the desire for conquest of the world. Jesus came to conquer the world to his sceptre, but by a method new to the universe by "losing his life" instead of "saving it." He penetrated the subtle assault of Satan at this point by the plain command, "Thou shalt have no other gods before me." So simple loyalty to God will penetrate the mists of many a dark assault of the devil, and open a plain and safe path for our feet.

Lastly, Satan assailed the desire for supernatural display-power and the show of it.

This desire for spiritual ornateness, for show of power, marvels, has caught many a soul and deflected it from the plain, safe path of holy living into the very showy one of marvels and peculiar divine demonstrations, until the "transformed angels of light" tripped their feet and they fell into the snare of the devil.

On the whole, we learn that Jesus' trial from Satan was just what a holy soul is subjected to. "He was tempted in all points as we are, yet without sin." That is, Christ having no depravity in His nature could not be tempted "with

His own lust," and so there is left only the field of temptation to which we are yet open when our depravity has been
removed. We see in Jesus the possibility with no probability of sinning. He could have given way, or there is
no meaning to the trial. But that He would give way
there was no probability. That mother with the babe in
her arms which she loves more than her own life, can de-
stroy it by her own hands. She has muscle strong enough
to choke it to death; it is a physical possibility; but so
long as mother-love reigns in her heart it is as safe in her
hands as in the hands of an angel. So "he that abideth
in Him sinneth not." He can sin so far as the volitional
possibility is concerned, but so long as he loves God with
all his heart, he will not. Jesus brought no power to bear
to overcome Satan that we may not bring to bear. So
we shall need yet to pray, "Lead us not into temptation
and deliver us from the Evil One."

There remains yet the second kind of trial to be considered, viz., trial for the sake of improvement. In the
sense of solicitation to evil, "God cannot be tempted, nor
tempteth He any man." His trial of us, whether direct,
or permissively, is always for our profit.

Refinement is after purification. Refinement is first to
increase our value to the kingdom of God. Take a piece

of crude iron, and by various processes of passing it through the fire it may be advanced from a value of ten cents a pound as crude iron, to hundreds of dollars a pound when by refinement it has been fitted for hair springs for watches. So while suffering has no sanctifying power, only Jesus' blood can do that, yet when the soul has been sanctified then the Masterhand can and does so manipulate the fires of trial that the soul comes thence seven times tried and increased in value in a ratio beyond our computation.

Again, trial of this sort is for usefulness. Take a piece of steel and forge a Damascus sword blade. Bring it to the exact size, shape, sharpness and polish, but it is yet good for nothing as a sword until it be tempered. Until then, if you strike an anakim, it will bend and likely stick the striker. But let the master put it in the fire until hot enough, and then suddenly transfer it to the water or oil until the proper tinge of color mark its whole length, and now you may strike with a force that bends your weapon double, but it springs back to its normal straightness and is ready in a moment for another stroke. You may put heavy weight upon it, and bend it down, but as soon as the weight is removed so soon will it straighten again. Now it is tempered. Now it is ready for service.

Now it is useful to the user. So, soul of mine, stand thou quiet in the fires until the Master shall have tempered and refined thee, that thou may'st be both useful and valuable to the King in His work.

X.

INFIRM.

Salvation is limited in us, here and now, by infirmities from which we may not be delivered until we reach the full fruition of the "glorious liberty of the sons of God" in the resurrection state. Infirmities are of two classes: physical and intellectual. The first Paul speaks of in Galatians 4: 13, "Ye know how through infirmity of the flesh I preached the gospel unto you at the first;" and the second in II Corinthians 4: 8, "We are troubled on every side, yet not distressed; we are perplexed, but not in despair."

Yet he declares in the 10th verse that he "always bears about the dying of the Lord Jesus that the life also of Jesus might be manifest in our body." Infirmities exist in the region of sensibilities and intellect, never in the will or affections. They are failures to keep the perfect law of obedience given to Adam in the garden of Eden. They are an involuntary outflow from an imperfect moral organism. They have their ground in our physical nature, and are aggravated by our intellectual deficiencies. They entail regret and humiliation, but in properly instructed

45

souls do not interrupt communion with God. Hidden from ourselves they are covered by the blood of Jesus. They are without remedy so long as we are in the body. We must learn to discriminate between infirmities and sins, which we may readily do by this simple line: Infirmities are involuntary, exist against our will. Sins are voluntary, and can originate only in the choice of our free will. Some earnest souls are much tormented by the "accuser of the brethren" with the idea that they have sinned without knowing it, or intending it. A wrong thing may have been done without our knowing it to be wrong—a thing we could not repeat without guilt; but if we did not know it to be wrong and did not intend to go counter to the Divine will, we have incurred no guilt. The act as a "falling short of the mark" has a certain element of sin in it, and needs the atonement, which, as the act of a child before the period of accountability, it has, and the act is covered by the atoning blood, and so gathers no guilt upon the soul.

Mistake in opinion or practice is not sin of such nature as to incur guilt. Yet every mistake is a violation of the perfect law of God, and this law cannot be broken without final recognition by God's government. Hence the mistake must be covered by the atonement, or it will expose the soul to death. In Numbers 15: 27, 28, we find provision made under Mosaism for meeting this case. And the Gospel has equal provision to meet the "sin of ignorance." Hence the presumption of those who imagine they do not need to pray, "Forgive us our trespasses." We constantly need the virtue of Christ's merit to cover our unintended lapses from the perfect law, and for failures from infirmities of flesh and spirit. The point then to be gained by the conscientious and devout follower of Jesus is to maintain an humble and watchful spirit with regard to infirmities, being careful not to repeat the mistakes which have been discovered to be such: and, on the other hand, not be driven from our moorings of a steady faith in the all-prevailing power of the blood, or shrink from our confident place in the "love of the Father." The enemy of our souls says to those who have made mistakes, "Now stay away from Jesus until you have shown ample sorrow and humility for the wrong," but Jesus says, "For we have not an high priest which cannot be touched with the feeling of our infirmities; but was in all points tempted like as we are, yet without sin. Let us therefore come boldly unto the throne of grace, that we may obtain mercy, and find grace to help in time of need."—Heb. 4: 15, 16. Thus while purity of heart does not give exemption from errors of judgment or mistakes in practice, it will give us the best use of what brain-power we have.

XI.

STABILITY.

The divine intention and normal state of salvation is that of establishment in the life of faith on the Son of God. "The Lord shall establish them an holy people unto Himself, as He has sworn unto thee, if thou shalt keep the commandments of the Lord thy God, and walk in His ways."—Deut. 28: 9. Obedience and progressive harmony with the Holy Spirit thus are the price and pathway of stability. Yet many persons get into the life of full salvation and drift out. What are prominent causes of this lapse from the higher states of grace?

1. A want of definite, clear Scriptural experience of perfect love. Many have not been clear in the first stages of Christian life, and when aroused upon the matter of entire sanctification they begin to seek, and after much heart sifting they get a better experience, but an honest analysis discovers it to be but an experience of justification. Others do not get to the bottom of entire consecration so thoroughly as to enable them to make a confident advance of faith in claiming this heritage of heart cleansing, and

so, though they have in greater or less degree what John Wesley called the "serenity of the philosopher," yet they do not have a clear, Scripturally attested, knowledge of heart-cleansing by the blood.

2. Others begin their life of holiness on a high tide of sense-life. While feeling is not to be ignored, but enjoyed in its proper place, and to be expected in every genuine experience of salvation, yet the basis of the life is "faith on the Son of God."—II Cor. 5: 7. Feeling varies, faith is constant. Feeling is enjoyable, but not essential, but without faith we cannot get on at all. Even the testimony of the Spirit to justification or entire sanctification is not feeling. It is the illumination of the mind as to a fact. The fact, purity by the blood, and the inabiding of the Holy Ghost produce feeling. Feeling is a consequence of conditions, not the condition itself. A locomotive standing quietly on the track with steam up and all ready to be attached to a train has just as much power as when she is thundering over the track at the head of an express train at sixty miles an hour. The only difference between the standing and the flying engine is that the latter has the power turned on the wheels. So, a Spirit-filled soul may be as truly filled with power from on high, while the body is quietly resting on a bed of

recuperation, as when in the midst of greatest activities in the work of Christ.

Again, we are satisfied that repeated cases demonstrate that many fail of stability in holiness because of failure freely, frankly and steadily to confess Jesus in all His offices. All the reasons for confession of Jesus at the earlier stages of the Christian life hold good as we advance to the higher stages of the same life. "Had we not better live our religion than say so much about it" has caught many a soul. The fallacy of this advice lies in the fact that the hidden springs of victory brought into "the soul that on Jesus relies" cannot be shown by any act or series of acts we can live before our friends or enemies. These springs can be known to the world only by the testimony of your tongue. Whatever our philosophy, experience shows first that it is instinctive and spontaneous for a soul to tell the glad story of full salvation, and, secondly, experience demonstrates that they who withhold the testimony, almost if not always, "soon have nothing about which to tell of the fullness of love."

Lastly, many fail of stability for want of activity. The life of holiness is an intensively active life. The Spirit which moved in creation, and every dispensation since, is a mighty energy and ceaseless moving power. We cannot retain his fellowship without a life of activity in the field where he is working. The seraphim of Isaiah's vision, with six winged furnishing, and voices never ceasing, cried "Holy, holy, holy is the Lord of Hosts, the whole earth is full of His glory." All along the line of Christ's greatest desire for laborers in the mission and slums, in the ministry and evangelistic field, in foreign field and home-place of quiet but constant endeavor, the hosts of holiness are pressing to the front with a zeal as quenchless as the fires of love, and a persistent purpose to glorify Him in constant activity.

XII.

SCARE-CROWS.

However it should have come to pass that a life of holiness should have come to be looked upon and talked of as a sort of sidetrack, or, at least, unusual thing, we may not fully say, but so it is. How common to hear the remark, "Those holiness folks," as though all Christians were not fully committed to holiness as a doctrine and as a life. It is the chief theme of the Bible. It is more frequently commanded, prayed for, set forth, sung about, and every way presented than any other subject of the Bible. Still, how many at its first mention show signs of alarm. It is said, "It divides the church." That may be in its favor or against it, dependent upon how it "divides the church." The prayer-meeting and class-meeting divide the church—the really spiritual, prayer-loving and Christian communion-loving from the unspiritual and cold-hearted professor. Yet, we do not condemn the prayer- and class-meetings for that. "Yes," says the objector, "I mean it makes them schismatic and intractable." Well, schismatic people, whose schism is that they will not mix the church and the world, will constantly appreciate spiritual rather than perfunctory services, and decide questions of church-engagement rather from a spiritual than a policy side; such so-called schism is to be commended rather than condemned. But while some may become schismatics in a bad sense who march in the holiness ranks, yet we must insist that other some, and they the great body of confessors of holiness, are the highest conservators of a genuine spiritual unity in the church. They are on hand at prayer-meeting and class. They stand by and uphold the preacher, and are his real spiritual bodyguard. Looking over the whole history of the church militant, we must declare that, as a body, on the whole, this cry is not true. It is a scare-crow.

"If we hold up so high a standard we shall discourage sinners." When you examine this objection carefully it is difficult to find the particular sinner who has been thus disheartened. But if some have, we are persuaded we can find an equal number who declare "That is just the Gospel I want," and "That is religion straight," and like expressions, which show the Gospel of full salvation "commends itself to every man's conscience in the sight of God."

"But it will discourage young converts." Not if what they have agrees with them. It would as likely discourage

a healthy, growing, school-boy who had had a good breakfast, and then running to school, had studied hard, played
hard, and ran all the way home, to tell him there was a
bigger dinner awaiting him than the breakfast he disposed of four and a half hours since. No, the religion of
Jesus agrees with itself, and he who enjoys what he has
will not object to more. This, too, is a scarce-crow.

"But a high profession endangers the cause, if any
do not come up to the standard." Well, a Christian cannot avoid a high profession. We all made a high profession when we were baptized, at the beginning of our
Christian profession. We then and there declared: "I
renounce the devil and all his works, the vain pomp and
glory of the world, with all covetous desires of the same,
and the carnal desires of the flesh, so that I will not fol-
low or be led by them." Also, I declared before the
church and the world that "I would endeavor, God being
my helper, to obediently keep God's holy will and commandments, and walk in the same all the days of my life."

So that we are in for a "high profession" if we have the
Christian profession at all. There is no low Christian profession. Again, this objection seems to emphasize our part
only, and leave God out of the count. We cannot stand by
our unaided effort, but "God is able to keep that which we

commit to Him unto that day." The effort to avoid responsibility by not making a high profession will not work. God sets the standard and will hold us to it whether we openly agree to obey or not. He does not ask us to sign the ten commandments before He will hold us responsible under them. This, also, is a scarce-crow.

XIII.

VERDICT.

The common-sense jury bring in this decision: We, the jury in the case of full salvation by two epochal experiences now obtained by consecration and faith in the atonement of Jesus Christ vs. general doubt and positive denial, decide in favor of the plaintiff under the following counts, to wit:

1. The evidence shows, with no rebutting testimony, that such full salvation is the ought-to-be of a complete system. Men ought to be saved from all sin.

2. The evidence goes to show, with no positive testimony to the contrary, but a great mass of testimony for said position, that there is such a state as entire sanctification, consisting of deliverance from the inbeing of the carnal mind, and the inabiding of the fullness of the Holy Spirit as the permanent occupant of the cleansed soul.

3. While a few testified that they "verily believed" that such a state was introduced by regeneration, and then perfected by slow stages of growth; and others testified they "verily believed" such a state could not be obtained until at or near death; yet each of these verily believing

theorists could adduce no clear testimony of those who know they reached this blessed rest of faith by these routes. On the other hand, a "great cloud of witnesses" testified they had reached, lived in, and enjoyed this Beulah-land-life for a number of years. Hence, this count was given to the side of the plaintiff.

4. The testimony goes to show that as clearly as men may know their sins forgiven, through faith in the atoning merit of Jesus' sacrifice, just so clearly may they know they have been delivered from the carnal mind, filled with the Holy Ghost and walk therein "before the Lord all the days of their lives."

5. The jury find that the testimony for the plaintiff is by such witnesses, as to their general character for truth and veracity, that had it been given by the same parties, in any court of justice, in a case of charged murder against the alleged criminal, the arrested party would have been surely hanged. On the other hand, the defence relied upon certain "metaphysical," and it was claimed "logical conclusions," upon which there was no general agreement, and which, to the jury, could not be seriously entertained in the face of the harmonious and united testimony of the evidence for the plantiff.

6. Though strong and persistent effort was put forth

by attorneys for the defence to break the chain of testimony, and bring discredit upon the witnesses, yet did their asservations stand the most taxing cross-examination, and we were the more convinced at every stage of the progress of the case of the sincerity of the witnesses, and the truthfulness of their assertions. Moreover, it was apparent to the jury that the witnesses had nothing to gain, so far as wordly emolument or popularity was concerned, by the testimony they gave, but, on the contrary, they, by their testimony, continually exposed themselves to a running fire of epithets, such as "cranks," "fanatics," etc., which to the natural man was anything but pleasant to endure. Yet they gave their testimony with faces that gleamed with the fire of love for truth and the cause of Him whom they served, which affected even many bystanders so that they declared "these men to be the servants of the most high God."

Lastly, we, the jury in above cause, find that by the plain and simple and unequivocal teaching and mandate of the Bible commanding us to "be holy"—by the commendation of this truth to every man's conscience in the sight of God—by the testing of a large company of men and women embracing all classes of intellect and social position in society from reformers, apostles, bishops, preachers, teachers, professors in colleges and universities to men and women in the commonest walks of life, from lords and ladies, wealthy and poor people, all agreeing through a series of centuries that there is such a life, and they enjoyed it, of freedom from the carnal mind, by entire consecration and faith in the blood of Jesus. Hence, we unanimously agree in this, our verdict, for the plantiff in this cause.

XIV.

MY SEAL.

"He that hath received his testimony hath set to his seal that God is true."—John 3: 33.

I was of Quaker parentage and had a mother of devout piety and eminent conscientiousness. She early taught me to pray, and so led me into the knowledge of God, so that at an early period, I think by the time I was five years of age, I had a clear sense of the favor of God and of fellowship with Him in prayer, which I very much enjoyed at many periods. I also felt I should preach the gospel, and at this early age had many very serious meditations thereon as my life work. In early manhood I left home, and in new associations and besetments I ceased regular prayers and gradually declined from my early religious position. After marriage, having become very wild and worldly in spirit, at twenty-four years of age, wife and I were both converted at a Methodist meeting. At once my early conviction that I should preach came back with renewed force. In fact, this was one of the things I had to settle in submitting to God in order to find peace with Him. "Immediately I conferred not with flesh and blood," save to tell my wife of my conviction, and she did not then, nor for thirty-seven years since, has she ever thrown a single obstacle, great or small, in my way in this ministry. The church gave outlet to the call and set me at work at once, as a happy young Christian, telling "what a dear Saviour I had found," verbally licensed by the church before my probationary period expired. Less than three months from my conversion I attended my first Quarterly Meeting in the Methodist Episcopal Church, and the Presiding Elder preached on "Perfect Love." I grew very hungry before the sermon was over. I retired from the place of meeting with great heart-searching and desire. I was not under condemnation as before my conversion. I could look up and pray with a consciousness of heart grip and sense of the divine presence and recognition I did not have at the threshold. But such was my sense of need, of want of inner likeness to God, of fetters on my spiritual life, that for three days and nights I could sleep but little. My struggle culminated on Sunday morning as I was going out to preach as a happy, young, verbally-licensed preacher. I had been on the stretch all night. I had been praying "Lord take me, take me, and perfect me in love." All at once it seemed like a sweet voice said "Why not step over and say, Lord keep me." At once I did change my prayer, and began to exercise faith in God's disposition to sanctify me wholly then, and light streamed in on my soul. I went on my way rejoicing and preached on perfect love with great freedom and joy. I entered the Conference—Des Moines—and for several years this was the central theme of my ministry. But with increas-ing responsibilities, position, and surroundings, and specially the influence of some of my older brethren in the ministry I began to tone down. I preached less upon per-fect love, and ceased to testify definitely to what God had wrought in my heart, and I went into an eclipse of my faith, and had years of wilderness life. I will not say these were entirely barren years; as a minister I was always hardworking and God gave gracious results. Revivals, churches and parsonages built, and all that goes to make up the visible results of a hardworking, diligent ministry was mine. Eight years of hard work in the Presiding Eldership helped to fill up these years. Nor were they years of heart-barrenness altogether. Many gracious re-vivals, many periods when my heart was flooded with grace —sometimes very near when I had been in heart-walk with God, but then, alas, periods when my soul was barren and heedless of its real state with God.

I became absorbed in visible results, which so many

called "success." Positions of increasing influence and responsibility were opened to me. Twice I was sent to the chief council of the Church as a delegate to General Conference. I returned to my pastoral charge from the last of them, the General Conference of 1884, sick at heart of mere place and position in the ministry. I longed for the old heart-life of my early ministry. All else seemed so hollow and tasteless without this. I began searching my heart. I would go to my study, open my Bible, and getting on my knees read and plead with God to "restore unto me the joy of His salvation and uphold me by His free spirit." Looking back now I can see that the blessed Holy Spirit had been preparing, both my wife and me, for this great epoch in our soul-life, for two years immediately previous to this time. He had set our experiences of justification into the clearest and happiest light we had enjoyed for years. He had blessed our labors with the salvation of souls and a very marked advance in the spirituality of our ministry. But, as I said above, I was very hungry for the restoration of the early freedom and joyous inward consciousness of full salvation that stood up in the memory of the first years of my life as a precious picture, now, alas, not a satisfying reality.

For a period, I judge, of six weeks I did nothing, save

attend to the necessary work of my ministry, but go to my
study every morning and spend the day, and sometimes a
good share of the night, in digging for the bottom of my
heart-relation to God. Oh, the heart-searchings the Holy
Spirit led me into. It seemed to me I had never realized
such mammoth caves and subterranean passages in my
nature as I did during that period of God searching in my
heart-life. Not of the same kind as the struggle of conviction of sin I had undergone previous to my conversion.
Yet the agony of desire of deep heart-hunger, of crying
out after the living God, I had never had before. My first
experience of hunger preceding my sanctification in the
beginning of my ministry had been deep and earnest, but
that whole experience seemed now, as I recalled it, to have
been so easy, a going over the short route by Kadesh
Barnea on the easy level of the normal approach to
Canaan. But now I had been making so many circuits in
the wilderness that I was, indeed, "entangled in that desert
land," and scarce knew how to take reckoning and make
any headway. But after weary marches and untellable
heart searchings and humiliations, one memorable Saturday evening I struck bed rock, and I knew, and I knew
God knew, I was at the bottom and all emptied out for
God possession. I did not have immediate jubilee as in my

first experience in entering Canaan. I felt as though I was attending a funeral. Deep, solemn, graveyard quiet came in, and I said, "It is done. I am all the Lord's. He and I know it." Looking back to the old experience I did not think I was at the end yet. But my now honest and earnest soul said, What shall I now do? The answer of my Bible and of my common sense was, "Believe on the Lord Jesus Christ." Well, what do I mean by "Believing on the Lord Jesus Christ?" Why, I mean that I will rise from this place of battle, and going out from this study, I will from this time forth do everything upon the basis of God's sure word: "If we walk in the light as He is in the light we have fellowship one with another, and the blood of Jesus Christ His Son cleanseth us from all sin." I immediately grasped this portion of truth, and began to make it the working basis of my life, moment by moment. For one week it seemed the adversary of my soul contested every step of my life. His chilly breath would seem to penetrate my very soul with the insinuation "You are not sanctified." But I was down to one thing. I had fought myself out on every other line. So I said at every point, place, and period of the day and waking hours of the night "The blood of Jesus Christ His Son cleanseth me from all sin." I will, I do believe it, and I will and do believe nothing else. Before the week was ended, though it had been a week of conflict sore and dire assault on my soul, yet I began to rejoice that I was still persistent, and had not lost, if I had not gained, any ground of spiritual advance. On the second Sunday after the Saturday evening's settlement, having three times preached to my people of the full gospel, and told them at the close "I was wholly the Lord's," and the "blood of Jesus cleansed me from all sin," I had ceased to look for any break or inundation of soul, feeling I had fooled away my former experience, and being so completely whipped out as to have nothing to ask, I went into class after morning sermon. The old class leader broke down in opening the meeting. His wife rose to testify, and God sanctified her as quick as flashing light. Several others were blessed, and some got under such conviction as to run out. I sat there a seeming spectator, almost indifferent to what was transpiring, when all at once my heart was broken up and a conflict of emotions like Paul's shipwrecking experience at Melita, "two ways met" in my heart: joy and tears, and I laughed and cried at once, scarcely able to tell which emotion was uppermost. For weeks this tide of emotion, tears and laughter, ebbed and flowed in my soul. I had emotion to spare. Enough for a whole family. What a luxury of tears! I never knew it was so delightful to cry. I had had a long dry spell, and my soul drank in the shower as a "dry and thirsty land." Then, how blessed to laugh! Well, if you have been there you know how it is; and if you have not, words will not convey it to your soul.

Gradually the emotion settled down into a steady substratum of life. Now on my fifteenth year in this blessed life I look back. Have I always been true and had no break whatever? No, I will not say that. But I will say there has been a steadiness of victory, a constancy of the availability of faith in the all cleansing blood, a persistence of keeping power preserving me in the knowledge and love of God, so much more satisfactory and blessed than before this period that it has seemed to me again and again I should deliberately choose rather to die than go back for a day, or a week, to the old state of soul-attitude to Jesus, my Saviour.

I believe I can say to the glory of my gracious Saviour, He has so kept me that for no whole day during the fifteen years have I been unconscious of His fully saving me from all sin. These have not been years of easy-going outer life. My soul, as to its moorings in Jesus, has undergone trials these years, compared with which the testings of all former years seem but skirmishes, while there have been Gettysburgs and Pittsburg Landing battles. But grace has been sufficient. In all these, and through them all, the conviction has grown, "I am persuaded He is able to keep that I've committed unto Him until that day."

How clear He has made my spiritual skies! The verities of spiritual entities stand out with a distinctness of outline that is like the portrait of a vast mountain against the clear, blue, cloudless sky beyond. How he has stood by me in trial and testing hours. So true and steadfast that it seems to me now there is no soul in the universe I know so well and who knows me so well as Jesus my Saviour. I gladly set my seal to the truth: "He is able to save them to the uttermost who come unto God by Him." Amen!

www.ingramcontent.com/pod-product-compliance
Lightning Source LLC
Chambersburg PA
CBHW020253090426
42735CB00010B/1910